HAVE
FAITH ANYWAY

HAVE
FAITH ANYWAY

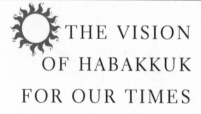

THE VISION
OF HABAKKUK
FOR OUR TIMES

Kent M. Keith

JOSSEY-BASS
A Wiley Imprint
www.josseybass.com

Published by Jossey-Bass
A Wiley Imprint
989 Market Street, San Francisco, CA 94103-1741 — www.josseybass.com

Readers should be aware that Internet Web sites offered as citations and/or sources for further information may have changed or disappeared between the time this was written and when it is read.

Jossey-Bass books and products are available through most bookstores. To contact Jossey-Bass directly call our Customer Care Department within the U.S. at 800-956-7739, outside the U.S. at 317-572-3986, or fax 317-572-4002.

Jossey-Bass also publishes its books in a variety of electronic formats. Some content that appears in print may not be available in electronic books.

Library of Congress Cataloging-in-Publication Data

Keith, Kent M.
    Have faith anyway : the vision of Habakkuk for our times / Kent M. Keith.
        p. cm.
    Includes bibliographical references.
    ISBN 978-0-470-28628-9 (cloth)
    1. Bible. O.T. Habakkuk–Criticism, interpretation, etc. I. Title.
    BS1635.52.K45 2008
    224'.9506–dc22

                                                            2008021036

Printed in the United States of America
FIRST EDITION
HB Printing   10 9 8 7 6 5 4 3 2 1

 CONTENTS

To the Reverend John Bolin, S.M.,
wise counselor and good friend

 PREFACE

I find it harder and harder to read the newspaper or watch the news. There are so many reasons to be discouraged about our world—wars, genocide, millions starving, climatic change, environmental degradation, threats of pandemics. And the Cold War may be over, but there are still enough nuclear weapons to kill every person on the planet.

What does it mean to have faith in a world that often seems headed for final destruction? What are we supposed to do to fulfill God's purposes?

The prophet Habakkuk provided us with insights that can help each of us think about these questions and search for our own answers. The Old Testament book that he wrote 2,600 years ago in a time of crisis and danger for the Hebrews is highly relevant today. It is a book about Habakkuk's struggle to understand what God was doing, and it is a book of extraordinary faith.

Habakkuk had a vision of a conversation with God. It was a vision about what God planned to do about the violence and injustice in Judah. God's plans included the destruction of Judah by a foreign power. Habakkuk had faith and trusted God even in the face of devastation and death. Nothing could stop him from rejoicing in the Lord. His vision is a magnificent aid to our own understanding of faith, as well as the perfect springboard for our own visions about the will of God and the future of our planet.

I was barely aware of the book of Habakkuk before my friend, the Reverend Don Asman, called it to my attention. "I want to show you something," he said, as he pulled out his pocket computer with its complete copy of the Bible. What he showed me was the last three verses of the book of Habakkuk:

> Though the fig tree does not bud
>> and there are no grapes on the vines,
> though the olive crop fails
>> and the fields produce no food,
> though there are no sheep in the pen
>> and no cattle in the stalls,

yet I will rejoice in the Lord,
  I will be joyful in God my Savior.
The Sovereign Lord is my strength;
  he makes my feet like the feet of a deer,
  he enables me to go on the heights.

The three verses resonated with me because they have the same spirit as the ten Paradoxical Commandments that I wrote in 1968, when I was a college sophomore. The commandments were part of a booklet I wrote for student leaders titled *The Silent Revolution*. I created the Paradoxical Commandments to help student leaders focus on finding personal meaning, even when the going gets tough. I told them that if they had the meaning, they didn't have to have the glory.

After the booklet was published, people started sharing the Paradoxical Commandments with others. They put the commandments up on their walls, passed them along to their friends, put them into speeches, and published them in books. Today it is estimated that the commandments have been used by millions of people all over the world.

I think there are several reasons that the Paradoxical Commandments continue to spread around the world.

First, they focus on finding meaning, and people are hungry for meaning. Second, they are not about the doctrines that divide us but about the fundamental values that we have in common as human beings. Third, they are short and easy to share. Fourth, they aren't suggestions; they are *commandments*. They challenge people to do the right thing. No excuses.

In 1997, I learned that Mother Teresa had put the Paradoxical Commandments up on the wall of her children's home in Calcutta. That discovery changed my life. It seemed to me that God was sending me a message. I felt called to speak and write about the Paradoxical Commandments again, three decades after I first published them.

I have often been asked, if you were to write the Paradoxical Commandments today, would you add any to the list? For years, I have resisted this idea. The commandments are guidelines for finding personal meaning in the face of adversity. The specific commandments aren't meant to cover all the situations that we face in life. They are examples of the *attitude* we need when we face those situations. We need to love people and help people and do what is right and good and true, no matter what the world does to us. We need to do it *anyway*. That's how we will find meaning and deep happiness—the kind of happiness that touches the spirit and connects with the soul.

I discussed the last three verses of Habakkuk with my wife, Elizabeth, who immediately understood the connection with the Paradoxical Commandments. She gave me a big smile and said, "You've found a new Paradoxical Commandment." I knew she was right. Here it is:

> THE WORLD IS FULL OF VIOLENCE, INJUSTICE,
> STARVATION, DISEASE, AND ENVIRONMENTAL
> DESTRUCTION. HAVE FAITH ANYWAY.

This book is about what we can learn from Habakkuk about how to have faith even when our world seems headed for disaster. It is about trying to understand how God is using the present situation— one that is bewildering and discouraging—to bring about his kingdom. It is about praying and discerning and acting in ways that will fulfill God's purposes.

In the pages ahead, we will read together the entire text of the Old Testament book of Habakkuk, seeking to understand and apply his vision and his faith. We will review the historical situation in his day and discuss his anguish, which is so similar to the anguish we experience in our own time. We will look at what it means to live in God's time, not our own. We will review the five "woes" that describe how leaders and nations should not behave. We will discuss the meaning of faith, what it is like to live a life of faith, and how to build a faith as unshakable as the faith of Habakkuk. We will conclude by asking, if a Christian were to have a vision today like the vision Habakkuk had 2,600 years ago, what would it be like?

After studying and praying on the book of Habakkuk, I was blessed to have my own vision. It consisted of words—separate blocks of dialogue between a Christian and God that I arranged into a single conversation. That vision is recorded in Chapter Nine. Receiving that vision was one of the most exciting experiences of my life. I encourage you to do what I did—to study and pray on the book of Habakkuk and be open to receiving your own vision.

We know that our world has truly become a fearful place. But if we have faith, we can stay connected with God and live the way Jesus taught us to live. We can love each other, help each other, and respect each other as the children of God. We can come together and build a new world. It will not be easy, but as we move forward, we can be inspired by the example of Habakkuk. He showed us that whatever happens, we can rejoice in the Lord and *have faith anyway*.

THE PARADOXICAL COMMANDMENTS

1. People are illogical, unreasonable, and self-centered.
   Love them anyway.

2. If you do good, people will accuse you of selfish ulterior motives.
   Do good anyway.

3. If you are successful, you will win false friends and true enemies.
   Succeed anyway.

4. The good you do today will be forgotten tomorrow.
   Do good anyway.

5. Honesty and frankness make you vulnerable.
   Be honest and frank anyway.

6. The biggest men and women with the biggest ideas can be shot down by the smallest men and women with the smallest minds.
   Think big anyway.

7. People favor underdogs but follow only top dogs.
   Fight for a few underdogs anyway.

8. What you spend years building may be destroyed overnight.
   Build anyway.

9. People really need help but may attack you if you do help them.
   Help people anyway.

10. Give the world the best you have and you'll get kicked in the teeth.
    Give the world the best you have anyway.

And now:

11. **The world is full of violence, injustice, starvation, disease, and environmental destruction.**
    Have faith anyway.

HAVE
FAITH ANYWAY

CHAPTER I

The Prophet Who Confronted God

Often when people of faith look at all the violence, injustice, starvation, disease, and environmental destruction in the world, they ask themselves, where is God? How can God allow this?

These important questions have been asked for literally thousands of years. They were asked with special eloquence by a Hebrew prophet named Habakkuk 2,600 years ago. Habakkuk had a vision in which he asked God these questions, and he got some answers. They were not the answers he wanted. But he responded with an affirmation of faith that stands out as one of the most beautiful passages in the Bible.

THE PROPHET HABAKKUK

We know very little about Habakkuk other than the words of the Old Testament book that he wrote. We do not know his tribe or hometown. The word *Habakkuk* may mean "embrace," as in a hug or enfolding that can keep you warm when there is no other shelter or source of warmth. Or it may have been an Akkadian or Babylonian name for a kind of garden plant or fruit tree. We don't know.[1] However, based on his writings, scholars estimate that Habakkuk lived at the end of the seventh century B.C., the same time period as the prophets Nahum, Zephaniah, and Jeremiah.[2]

The book of Habakkuk begins with the words "The oracle that Habakkuk the prophet received" (Hab. 1:1).[3] When a prophet received an oracle, it was his responsibility to communicate it to God's people. In Habakkuk's case, the task was especially difficult, since the message was that the kingdom of Judah would be destroyed by the Babylonians.

The traditional role of the prophet was to call the people back to a right relationship with God. When the people drifted away from their covenant with God, the prophets would urge them to repent and become obedient again. As you might expect, it was an unpopular role. Prophets were often attacked by those they called to repentance.

Habakkuk was a different kind of prophet. Instead of confronting his people, he confronted God. He wanted to know what God was doing to fulfill his covenant with his people. How could God allow so much violence and injustice? How could God allow his covenant to be broken without doing anything about it?

A TURBULENT TIME

Habakkuk lived during a turbulent time for the Judeans. After the reign of King Solomon, Israel split into two kingdoms—the northern kingdom of Israel and the southern kingdom of Judah. The two kingdoms were dominated and eventually destroyed as the Assyrians then the Egyptians, and finally the Babylonians assumed control of the region.

The Assyrians conquered the northern kingdom of Israel in 722–721 B.C. The tribes of Israel were assimilated into other cultures or were deported. The Assyrians invaded the southern kingdom of Judah in 701 B.C., destroying many cities but leaving Jerusalem unharmed. Judah survived as a vassal of Assyria, allowed to govern its own internal affairs but paying heavy tribute and taxes to the Assyrians.

Judah became more independent toward the end of the reign of King Josiah (640–609 B.C.). King Josiah launched internal reforms and expanded Judah's territory and influence to the north. Meanwhile, tribes from southern Babylonia known as Chaldeans took over the Babylonian Empire and expanded it. These "Neo Babylonians" defeated the main Assyrian force in battle in 612 B.C.

With the defeat of the Assyrians, the Egyptians saw an opportunity. In 609 B.C., the Egyptians marched through Judah on their way to do battle with the Babylonians. King Josiah tried to stop them and was killed in the battle. Judah became a vassal of the Egyptians, who placed Jehoiakim on the throne. King Jehoiakim was known as a petty tyrant who allowed pagan practices and the deterioration of public morality.

The situation changed a few years later, in 605 B.C., when the Bablyonians defeated Egypt at Carchemish. The Babylonians were now the only major power in the region. Some time around 603 B.C., as the Babylonian army advanced toward

Judah, King Jehoiakim conceded and became a vassal of the Babylonians.[4]

However, Jehoiakim later rebelled against the Babylonians. As a result, in 598–597 B.C., the Babylonian army marched on Judah, arriving in Jerusalem just after Jehoiakim died. The new king, Jehoiachin, surrendered. In order to subjugate the kingdom, the Babylonians took Jehoiachin, his wives, his servants, the queen mother, high officials, and thousands of leading citizens, soldiers, and craftsmen to Babylon.[5] The Babylonians placed Zedekiah on the throne of Judah.

There was continuing unrest in Judah. When a rebellion broke out in 589 B.C., the Babylonians' response was harsh. They blockaded Jerusalem and two years later conquered the city, burning it down and leveling its walls. The Babylonians then proceeded to destroy the cities of Judah, killing many people and ruining the economy. They did not stop until the kingdom of Judah was no more.[6]

When Judah was destroyed, more Judeans were carried off to Babylon. The "Babylonian exile" continued until Persia conquered Babylonia in 539–538 B.C. The Persian leader, Cyrus the Great, allowed the Judeans to return to their homeland.

THE BOOK OF HABAKKUK

The book of Habakkuk was probably written sometime during the reign of Jehoiakim, who ruled from 609 to 598 B.C.[7] That was after the fall of the Assyrians and before Jerusalem was destroyed by the Babylonians. The coming invasion by the Babylonians was revealed to Habakkuk in his vision, as was the fall of the Babylonians at the hands of the Persians many years later.

The book of Habakkuk has three chapters. In the first two chapters, Habakkuk makes two complaints, each of which God answers in turn. The third chapter is a prayer or psalm that recalls God's glory and is a powerful affirmation of faith.

We turn now to the vision of Habakkuk, his two complaints, and God's answers.

 CHAPTER 2

The Anguish of Habakkuk

Habakkuk loved God, but he was not happy with God. Things were not right. He turned to God and complained.

HABAKKUK'S FIRST COMPLAINT

Habakkuk's first complaint to God was about God's apparent inaction in the face of violence and injustice in Judah:

> How long, O Lord, must I call for help,
>   but you do not listen?
> Or cry out to you, "Violence!"
>   but you do not save?

Why do you make me look at injustice?
  Why do you tolerate wrong?
Destruction and violence are before me,
  there is strife, and conflict abounds.
Therefore the law is paralyzed,
  and justice never prevails.
The wicked hem in the righteous,
  so that justice is perverted. (Hab. 1:2–4)

Habakkuk had the courage to honestly ask the questions that were troubling him. He did not cry out because of a personal tragedy or loss. He was concerned about Judah. He knew that God does not approve of violence and injustice, but somehow, they were rampant in the land. Why? And how long must he cry for help? Why didn't God answer? Habakkuk did not doubt God, but he was filled with anguish. He wanted to know what God was doing.

We can understand the questions Habakkuk asked God, because they are our questions too. We too want to know why there is so much violence in the world. We remember the terrorist attacks in the United States and other nations, and we feel vulnerable to more attacks. There is continued tension between nations and between ethnic groups within nations. We have seen war in the Middle East. We have witnessed genocide in Bosnia, Rwanda, and Sudan. And there seems to be no end to the earthquakes, hurricanes, tsunamis, floods, and fires around the world that leave hundreds of thousands dead and many more homeless.

And why is there so much injustice? People in many countries are oppressed because of their race, religion, political beliefs, or gender. Why are some people wealthy while millions do not have enough to eat? All over the world, children go to bed hungry every night. Why do some people have access to education and health care while millions do not? So many people have no hope for a better future. They live in squalor and die of preventable diseases. The human immunodeficiency virus (HIV) has killed millions all over the world. In Africa alone, HIV/AIDS has made orphans of millions of children. Meanwhile, corruption among government and business leaders throughout the world seems as rampant as in the days of Habakkuk.

Like Habakkuk, we call on God to answer. What are you doing about this, God? Where are you? We don't understand. We don't see the divine plan. Our lives are much too filled with anguish.

GOD'S ANSWER TO HABAKKUK'S
FIRST COMPLAINT

God answered Habakkuk, revealing that the wicked would be punished. However, they would be punished in a way that would be a surprise to Habakkuk. God said:

> Look at the nations and watch—
> and be utterly amazed.
> For I am going to do something in your days
> that you would not believe,
> even if you were told.
> I am raising up the Babylonians,
> that ruthless and impetuous people,
> who sweep across the whole earth
> to seize dwelling places not their own.
> They are a feared and dreaded people;
> they are a law to themselves
> and promote their own honor.
> Their horses are swifter than leopards,
> fiercer than wolves at dusk.
> Their cavalry gallops headlong;
> their horsemen come from afar.

They fly like a vulture swooping to devour;
    they all come bent on violence.
Their hordes advance like a desert wind
    and gather prisoners like sand.
They deride kings
    and scoff at rulers.
They laugh at all fortified cities;
    they build earthen ramps and capture them.
Then they sweep past like the wind and go on—
    guilty men, whose own strength is their god.
    (Hab. 1:5–11)

God answered that he was indeed at work, but not in the way Habakkuk wanted or expected. God was raising the Babylonians to be his instrument of justice. The Babylonian army was ruthless, swift, and unstoppable. It would sweep across the earth and punish the people of Judah.

Habakkuk may have thought that God was doing nothing, because he did not *understand* what God was doing. Habakkuk didn't see the big picture. He didn't expect to learn that the response to the situation in his own nation would come from forces beyond Judah.

Not only was God's answer unexpected, but it was also a *fearful* answer. God told Habakkuk in his vision that the Judeans would be conquered by the ruthless Babylonians. The Judeans would no longer be prosperous or independent. They would be subjugated. They would be at the mercy of the wicked. In short, things would get a lot worse before they got better.

Sometimes we pray, expecting a certain answer or outcome, and are surprised by what we hear instead. We want God to do what *we* think is right instead of what *God* thinks is right. After all, we are the "good guys," and our plan is simple: we will win. But it doesn't always happen that way. God may say no. God may have another plan.

HABAKKUK'S SECOND COMPLAINT

Habakkuk was not satisfied with God's answer to his first complaint. He knew that God does not approve of evil; God doesn't tolerate wrong. Habakkuk therefore lodged his second complaint:

O Lord, are you not from everlasting?
    My God, my Holy One, we will not die.

O Lord, you have appointed them to execute
judgment;
  O Rock, you have ordained them to punish.
Your eyes are too pure to look on evil;
  you cannot tolerate wrong.
Why then do you tolerate the treacherous?
  Why are you silent while the wicked
  swallow up those more righteous than
  themselves? (Hab. 1:12–13)

Habakkuk's second complaint was that God was
going to use the wicked Babylonians to punish the
people of Judah, even though the people of Judah
were more righteous than the Babylonians. The
Judeans may have been wicked and violent, but the
Babylonians were surely far worse!

Habakkuk had another fear. Would the Babylonians
wipe out the Judeans? If so, the punishment would
far exceed the crime. Habakkuk was shocked. God
had made promises to Abraham, Isaac, and Israel;
the Judeans were their descendants, the people of the
covenant. Now it looked as though they might all die.
Habakkuk wanted reassurance.

Habakkuk used a metaphor to complain about
God's toleration of the treacherous and the wicked.

Habakkuk said that God had made people as helpless as fish in the sea, caught with the hooks and nets of their wicked enemies.

> You have made men like fish in the sea,
>> like sea creatures that have no ruler.
> The wicked foe pulls all of them up with hooks,
>> he catches them in his net,
> he gathers them up in his dragnet;
>> and so he rejoices and is glad.
> Therefore he sacrifices to his net
>> and burns incense to his dragnet,
> for by his net he lives in luxury
>> and enjoys the choicest food.
> Is he to keep on emptying his net,
>> destroying nations without mercy?
> (Hab. 1:14–17)

Habakkuk complained because he did not like God's methods, and he felt helpless. Like Habakkuk, we too may not like God's methods, or we may feel helpless, like fish caught up in the nets of the wicked. We do not understand how God works through human beings, through nations, to bring about God's will.

And like Habakkuk, we too face destruction and disaster. We look at the natural environment, and we see steady degradation. Poisonous chemicals are spreading; endangered species are dying; temperatures are rising; ice caps are melting; deserts are claiming regions that were once full of lakes and forests. In the decades to come, there may be massive flooding in coastal areas, affecting hundreds of millions of people throughout the world. Changes in world climates may make it harder for certain regions to produce food. Millions of people may have to migrate due to drought. Cities may have to be abandoned.

Meanwhile, we fear pandemics that could be almost unstoppable for lack of enough vaccine or the right kind of vaccine or drugs that can effectively treat the disease. And thousands of nuclear bombs still sit in their silos. It would take only one hundred of those nuclear bombs, exploding over cities, to create enough smoke to blanket the atmosphere and prevent the sun from shining through. This "nuclear winter" could kill all living things on our planet. Will nations be destroyed without mercy? Will we all die catastrophically? Our own questions echo the urgent questions of Habakkuk.

 CHAPTER 3

In God's Time, Not Our Time

After lodging his second complaint, Habakkuk waited patiently for God's answer. He said:

> I will stand at my watch
>   and station myself on the ramparts;
> I will look to see what he will say to me,
>   and what answer I am to give to this complaint.
>   (Hab. 2:1)

Habakkuk stood watch, like a sentry, waiting to see what God would say. He stationed himself on the ramparts, which were typically mounds of earth, often with stone parapets, that were raised as fortifications around ancient cities. When you stood on the ramparts, you could see whoever approached the city. It was a good

17

place to wait for the news that travelers and messengers might bring. We can imagine Habakkuk up on the ramparts, away from the hustle-bustle noise of the city, looking toward the countryside, quietly waiting.

While he waited, he was confident that God would answer him. He was looking forward to what God would say and to his own response to God's words.

> Then the Lord replied:
> "Write down the revelation
>   and make it plain on tablets
>   so that a herald may run with it.
> For the revelation awaits an appointed time;
>   it speaks of the end
>   and will not prove false.
> Though it linger, wait for it;
>   it will certainly come and will not delay."
>   (Hab. 2:2–3)

God answered Habakkuk by instructing him to write down what God was going to say. God wanted his words to be preserved so that they could sustain the Judeans in the future. God also wanted Habakkuk to wait for the revelation.[1] The revelation would come, but Habakkuk must be patient! He must remember that God's time is not human time.

What do we know of God's time? We can't imagine it. It is infinite. Whether we think that the universe began with a "big bang" billions of years ago or that the earth was created six thousand years ago, God's time is far beyond our understanding. God is not limited by human time.

Most of us are not good at waiting for God's time. We want God to act now. We want God to fulfill our own timetable. We want God to do what *we* think God should do, when *we* think God should do it. So we make announcements, confidently predicting what God's next move will be and how soon God will act. We think we know! Usually, we predict that God will do exactly what we want God to do, as though we were in control, not God!

We are not patient. We want things *now*. We don't want to wait in line; we want to be served immediately. We want our food to be prepared within five minutes. And we want our institutions to get results fast. Our businesses are expected to produce results every three months for the quarterly report, or we will sell our shares and call for new leadership. Our political leaders are expected to solve problems in time for the next election, or we will throw them out of office. We don't think in terms of decades or centuries, even though some solutions take that long. We are not content to take the first steps on a long journey. We are not willing to protect long-term investments in our future. If we plant a tree, we keep pulling it up to inspect its roots, and then we wonder why it grows so slowly.

Perhaps we are less patient today because technology has accelerated our sense of human time. Thousands of years ago, we measured time in days and nights. Then we invented clocks that made it possible to measure hours and minutes. Now every second counts. Five or ten seconds seems like a long time to us.

Meanwhile, we are too busy. We operate twenty-four hours a day, seven days a week, but we have no time! And with our cell phones, pagers, and e-mail, we have no time to ourselves.

We have even less time to be alone with God. So when God speaks to us, we may not be listening. We are in too much of a hurry. We are too focused on ourselves.

But it doesn't have to be that way. We can slow down and listen to God. We can do what Habakkuk did.

As we go through our daily lives, we can stop, and seek high ground. We can stand on the ramparts, watching and listening. We can be open to what God will say next. We can humbly wait for God to speak to us.

How does God speak to us? Through revelation. Through scripture. Through prayer. Through other people. Through the incidents and coincidences of our daily lives. If we are patient, we can learn to read "the signs of the times."

We know that whatever God decides to do, God will do in God's time, not ours. *Having faith in God means having faith in God's time.* It means trusting that God will do what God knows must be done when God decides it is the right time to do it. We may understand God's timing, or we may not; we may see the revelation fulfilled, or we may not. Like Habakkuk, we must preserve God's message and then wait for God's time.

CHAPTER 4

The Lessons of the Five Woes

Habakkuk stood watch, and God answered. God's answer to Habakkuk's second complaint was that the Babylonians will be judged. Their empire will fall. Tyranny, evil, and corruption will lead to the collapse of the Babylonian Empire.

God began his answer by describing someone who is proud or "puffed up." The person referred to in this passage may be the Babylonian king, but God's words can be used to describe anyone who behaves this way.[1]

> See, he is puffed up;
>> His desires are not upright—
>> But the righteous will live by his faith—

Indeed, wine betrays him;
    he is arrogant and never at rest.
Because he is as greedy as the grave
    and like death is never satisfied,
he gathers to himself all the nations
    and takes captive all the peoples. (Hab. 2:4–5)

God contrasted the "puffed up" person with the righteous person who lives by his faith. We will discuss that key phrase, "the righteous will live by his faith," in the next chapter.

God's answer to Habakkuk's second complaint included five "woes." The word translated as "woe" can also be translated as "alas" or "oh!" or "how terrible for them!"[2] The woes are against stealing and extortion; unjust gain and the ruin of others; bloodshed and crime; debauchery and violence; and trust in idols.[3] It is clear from the woes that the wicked Babylonians—and others who are like them—will eventually be punished. In the meantime, the woes give the Judeans words to use in taunting the Babylonians while the Judeans await deliverance from them. The words are in the form of a funeral dirge, to mock the Babylonians.[4]

THE FIVE WOES

The first woe is against stealing and extortion:

> Will not all of them taunt him with ridicule
>   and scorn, saying,
> Woe to him who piles up stolen goods
>   and makes himself wealthy by extortion!
>   How long must this go on?
> Will not your debtors suddenly arise?
>   Will they not wake up and make you tremble?
>   Then you will become their victim.
> Because you have plundered many nations,
>   the peoples who are left will plunder you.
> For you have shed man's blood;
>   you have destroyed lands and cities and
>   everyone in them. (Hab. 2:6–8)

The second woe is against unjust gain and the ruin of others:

> Woe to him who builds his realm by unjust gain
>   to set his nest on high,
>   to escape the clutches of ruin!

You have plotted the ruin of many peoples,
    shaming your own house and forfeiting
    your life.
The stones of the wall will cry out,
    and the beams of the woodwork will echo it.
    (Hab. 2:9–11)

The third woe is against bloodshed and crime:

Woe to him who builds a city with bloodshed
    and establishes a town by crime!
Has not the Lord Almighty determined
    that the people's labor is only fuel for the fire,
    that the nations exhaust themselves for nothing?
For the earth will be filled with the knowledge of
    the glory of the Lord,
    as the waters cover the sea. (Hab. 2:12–14)

The fourth woe is against debauchery and violence:

Woe to him who gives drink to his neighbors,
    pouring it from the wineskin till they are drunk,
    so that he can gaze on their naked bodies.
You will be filled with shame instead of glory.
    Now it is your turn! Drink and be exposed!

The cup from the Lord's right hand is coming
around to you,
and disgrace will cover your glory.
The violence you have done to Lebanon will
overwhelm you,
and your destruction of animals will
terrify you.
For you have shed man's blood;
you have destroyed lands and cities and
everyone in them. (Hab. 2:15–17)

The fifth woe is against trust in idols:

Of what value is an idol, since a man has carved it?
Or an image that teaches lies?
For he who makes it trusts in his own creation;
He makes idols that cannot speak.
Woe to him who says to wood, "Come to life!"
Or to lifeless stone, "Wake up!"
Can it give guidance?
It is covered with gold and silver;
there is no breath in it.
But the Lord is in his holy temple;
let all the earth be silent before him.[5]
(Hab. 2:18–20)

These words apply to the ancient Babylonians. They are also a warning to us today. We must make sure that we do not become the *new* Babylonians.

We must not extort others to become wealthy or plunder other nations or destroy lands and cities and everyone in them. We must not build our realm by unjust gain or plot the ruin of other peoples. We must not build cities with bloodshed or establish towns by crime. We must not promote drunkenness and violence. We must not become idolatrous. We must not worship our own strength, as the Babylonians worshiped theirs. God reminds us that if we do these things, we will ultimately be punished.

Of all the woes, idolatry may be our strongest temptation. Idolatry is worshiping anything other than God. We tend to worship the things we have made and the things we have purchased. For example, we seek the materialistic symbols of success—a big house, a fancy car, the latest technology, expensive clothes, the finest restaurants, and vacations at the most fashionable resorts.

This idolatry cannot make us happy, nor can it make us right with God. When we create and worship our own idols, we turn away from God. We forget to love God and love our neighbors as ourselves. Idolatry focuses us on our own strengths, as though we created them ourselves instead of receiving them as gifts.

We can create idols, but we did not create God. God created us. We are the children of the living God, and we should humbly worship God only. As Habakkuk reminds us, "the Lord is in his holy temple; let all the earth be silent before him."

 CHAPTER 5

Living by Faith

In God's answer to Habakkuk's second complaint, God said, "but the righteous will live by his faith." This phrase is quoted often. It has been called "one of the Old Testament statements which has had a profound influence on the history of the church."[1] Paul quoted it in Romans 1:17: "For in the gospel a righteousness from God is revealed, a righteousness that is by faith from first to last, just as it is written: 'The righteous will live by faith.'"

Again, at Galatians 3:11, Paul wrote, "Clearly no one is justified before God by the law, because, 'The righteous will live by faith.'" And the writer of the epistle to the Hebrews said, "But my righteous one will live by faith" (Heb. 10:38).

What is faith? Faith is trust and confidence in God.[2] It is believing in things unseen. As Paul wrote in 2 Corinthians 5:7, "We live by faith, not by sight." Hebrews 11:11 says that "faith is being sure of what we hope for and certain of what we do not see." Faith is about the things we see not physically but spiritually. If we can see it in a physical sense, we can prove its existence scientifically, and so we do not need faith.

A TRUSTING RELATIONSHIP

When we have faith, we know that God doesn't cease to exist just because times are tough. We know that while our own actions can make God happy or sad, nothing that we do, and nothing that anybody else says or does, can change the fact that God exists. God is there, loving us, and inviting us into a relationship with him.

And that's what it means to live by faith. It means having a trusting relationship with God. It means trusting God, even when you do not understand what God is doing.

Our relationship with God should be the kind of relationship that Habakkuk had with God—a mature two-way relationship. Habakkuk trusted God. He honored and obeyed God. But he wanted to know what God was doing and why. So he confronted God the way he would confront a beloved friend. He asked the questions that one asks in a trusting, personal relationship.

UP TO EACH OF US

Faith is our response to God's self-revelation. That is why faith is up to each of us—we are free to respond to God or not. When we choose to respond to God in faith, we begin a lifelong journey whose goal is eternal union with God. Growing in faith makes the journey meaningful and exciting.

Our faith can be strengthened from many sources— from the Bible, from the lives and teachings of people of faith, and from the wonders of the natural world around us. Faith can be enriched by any experience that reveals to us that there is something more, something beyond the materialistic world, something spiritual and transcendent and inspiring. We may experience our own revelations of God in moments of joy, peace, and love. We may also experience our own revelations in moments of despair, when we call on God to be with us in our pain.

Faith is not just personal; it is communal. We live our faith in community with others—our family, our church, and all of God's people. We can give each other the love and encouragement we need to keep our faith vibrant and strong.

FAITH AND GOD'S PRESENCE

When we live by faith, we live with a sense of God's presence. We are so aware of God that God's presence is almost tangible. We sense God; we feel God; we see God at work in our lives and the lives of those around us. When we sense God's presence, life becomes sacred.

We can see God in the amazing natural world God created. We live amid a hundred billion galaxies, each with billions of stars. We live in a cycle of rain and evaporation that allows vegetation to flourish and rivers to flow. Energy comes from the sun, a free gift to our planet each day, causing plants to grow, giving us food as well as seeds for new growth. We are highly complex human beings, but each of us began as a sperm cell and a microscopic egg. Life itself is a miracle.

We can see the Creator in dramatic yellow, orange, and pink sunsets, misty green mountains, bright white sand beaches, cool shadowy forests, clear lakes, and majestic snow-covered mountains. Nature fills us with wonder. Why do we feel so at peace in a forest and so inspired by the light that shines through the trees? Why does a clear, gurgling brook speak to our souls? Nature inspires us. Perhaps it is just one way that God reminds us that he is here and that the natural world that God created is sacred.

I like to see God in little things. For example, there is a rubber plant in the conference room at my office. It is about four feet tall, with branches reaching out in all directions, covered with big green leaves. It sits near the window, and gets some sunlight through the blinds. I give it water three times a week. What amazes me is that it not only lives but *grows*. It sent up a new shoot, with nine bright green leaves, beautifully proportioned, fresh and new. Then it sent up another one. I am filled with wonder. Just soil and water and sunlight, and fresh green shoots rise up and open out. It is a small thing, but it touches me. It is like God saying, "Watch this!" And I can only respond, "Wow!" I look at each new shoot, and I feel the freshness, the hope, the affirmation of life. God is there, even in the little things.

We can feel the presence of the Holy Spirit in the love we share with family and friends. We feel the Spirit in little acts of kindness, the shared happiness and sorrow, the unabashed caring between friends and colleagues. I feel the presence of the Holy Spirit in simple moments, such as the times when my family and I are all together, sitting at the dinner table, talking and laughing and teasing. It doesn't matter what we are talking or laughing or teasing about. What matters is that we are there, and so is the Holy Spirit.

We feel the presence of Christ when we are called to do more and to be more—to take up our crosses and carry them. We can be *in* the world, not *of* the world. We can do what we know is right and good and true, no matter what the world does to us. We can follow the example Jesus gave us on Good Friday. In the face of pain and cruelty and hate, Jesus loved people anyway. He forgave people anyway. And he saved people anyway. The world could not change who he was or what he came to do. We can feel his presence as we seek to live the paradoxical life that he lived.[3]

CONNECTING WITH THE HEALING POWER OF FAITH

Our faith connects us to the healing power of Christ. Jesus told those he healed that it was their faith that made the healing possible. For example, a woman who had been bleeding for twelve years came up behind Jesus and touched his cloak. She thought that if she could only touch his cloak, she would be healed. Jesus turned and saw her. "Take heart, daughter," he said, "your faith has healed you." And at that moment, she was healed (Matt. 9:20–22).

A short time later, Jesus healed two blind men. Jesus asked them, "Do you believe that I am able to do this?" They said yes. Jesus touched their eyes and said, "According to your faith will it be done to you." Their eyesight was restored (Matt. 9:27–30).[4]

Faith was the connection. Faith created the relationship. Faith opened the channel for Jesus to do his healing work. Faith made miracles possible.

Jesus wanted to make sure we know how important faith is. He made very bold statements about what is possible if we have faith. At Matthew 17:20, he said, "I tell you the truth, if you have faith as small as a mustard seed, you can say to this mountain, 'Move from here to there,' and it will move. Nothing will be impossible for you."[5] If it fits God's plan, God will make it happen.

FAITH AND FACTS

In our daily lives, we want the facts. We want to know who is doing what and why. We want to know how things work and which things work best. We want explanations. We don't like uncertainty. We always want proof. Sometimes we even want proof that God exists.

Perhaps this desire for facts and proof comes from the immense impact that science and technology have had on the way we think. Though we have benefited immensely from science and technology and have learned a lot by measuring and testing the material world, the life of faith is not about the material world. It is about the life of the spirit; it is about things unseen. Not everything can be measured and proved. Some things can only be perceived and believed.

Faith is about divine mysteries, revelation, and our relationship with God. Faith is a gift from God, a gift of the Spirit (1 Cor. 12:7–11; Gal. 5:22). Faith makes it possible for us to have a personal, continuing relationship with the three manifestations of God—the Father, Son, and Holy Spirit. That is why our faith can remain strong and give our lives meaning, no matter what is happening in the material world of facts and proofs.

In the end, there is something more important than proof of God, and that is *a relationship with God*. Only faith can make the relationship possible.

FULLY ALIVE IN FAITH

When we live in faith, we are fully alive. We acknowledge the gifts God has given us, and we want to use those gifts. We want our faith to flow into our deeds. We want to serve God by serving others. We accept the message of Jesus and commit to living that message. Jesus said, "I tell you the truth, anyone who has faith in me will do what I have been doing" (John 14:12). And James said:

> What good is it, my brothers, if a man claims to have faith but has no deeds? Can such a faith save him? Suppose a brother or sister is without clothes and daily food. If one of you says to him, "Go, I wish

you well; keep warm and well fed," but does nothing about his physical needs, what good is it? In the same way, faith by itself, if it is not accompanied by action, is dead. (James 2:14–17)

Like Habakkuk, our faith may be tested. We may face devastation and death. But James reminds us:

Consider it pure joy, my brothers, whenever you face trials of many kinds, because you know that the testing of your faith develops perseverance. Perseverance must finish its work so that you may be mature and complete, not lacking anything. (James 1:2–4)[6]

In Isaiah 7:9, the Lord said, "If you do not stand firm in your faith, you will not stand at all." Paul echoed that message when he told the Corinthians to "stand firm in the faith" (1 Cor. 16:13). He urged Timothy to "fight the good fight of the faith" (1 Tim. 6:11–12).

When we look back at the end of our lives, each of us will be blessed if we can say what Paul said in 2 Timothy 4:6–7:

For I am already being poured out like a drink offering, and the time has come for my departure. I have fought the good fight, I have finished the race, I have kept the faith.

 CHAPTER 6

Faith Versus Beliefs

Habakkuk knew what God had done for his people in the past. In the third chapter of his book, Habakkuk began his prayer:

> Lord, I have heard of your fame;
>   I stand in awe of your deeds, O Lord.
> Renew them in our day,
>   in our time make them known;
>   in wrath remember mercy. (Hab. 3:1–2)

Habakkuk was in awe of what God had done, and he wanted God to do great deeds again for the Judeans. But that is not what God was going to do. God told Habakkuk that he was raising the Babylonians *against* the Judeans. This was not what Habakkuk wanted to hear, nor was it what he wanted to believe. He wanted to believe that God would again be the warrior and champion of his people.

How could Habakkuk have such faith when he believed that God was going to do something very painful and destructive? How could Habakkuk have such unshakable faith when his beliefs about God were being challenged?

Perhaps the best answer is that *faith* and *beliefs* are not the same thing.[1] We use the two words interchangeably in our daily conversation, but it is helpful to distinguish them. The reason is that our faith can be unshakable, even while our beliefs change with new knowledge and spiritual growth.

CONFIDENCE AND TRUST IN GOD

We have good days and bad days. Things go well and not so well. We experience both joys and sorrows. God does not promise that we will never suffer; God promises that he will be with us, no matter what. So even when we experience calamities, our faith can still be strong. We can still be confident of God, and we can still trust God.

Habakkuk had confidence and trust in God. He learned of the coming destruction and said that even if everything goes wrong, he will still have faith in God. And he will do more than that—he will praise and rejoice in the Lord. His living relationship with God gave him joy, and his faith ensured that his relationship with God would continue.

BELIEFS ABOUT GOD

Faith is confidence and trust in God; a belief is a religious creed or doctrine. Our beliefs are *about* God, our attempts to describe the Father, the Son, and the Holy Spirit. So we have faith *in* God and beliefs *about* God.

There are approximately two hundred Christian denominations in the United States, and their beliefs about the Father, Son, and the Holy Spirit vary. For example, one denomination believes that the Holy Spirit played an active role in creation and is the agent of the new birth. Another denomination believes that the Holy Spirit is the Ruler of the world and the source of grace, regenerating and sanctifying the souls of believers. A third denomination believes that the

Holy Spirit convicts people of sin and empowers people for service. And a fourth denomination believes that the Holy Spirit is the living presence of God, joining believers together in brotherhood.[2] Each denomination describes the Holy Spirit in a different way.

Our beliefs about the Father, Son, and the Holy Spirit are important. However, our beliefs should not become the object of our faith. We need to remember that we worship God, not our beliefs about God.

When our beliefs become the object of our faith, two things can happen. First, we can cling so tightly to our beliefs that we shut ourselves off from new religious insights that might result in a revision of our beliefs and spiritual growth. We are not open to surprises, such as the surprise that Habakkuk received in answer to his complaints. He was surprised (and dismayed) that God decided to use the Babylonians to accomplish God's purposes.

The second thing that can happen when our beliefs become the object of our faith is that when we can no longer accept a certain belief, we may feel as though we are losing our faith. But our beliefs are not our faith. Old beliefs may fall away, and new beliefs may replace them, but *God is still God*. We can still have faith—we can still have confidence and trust in God—even if we change our descriptions of God.

Let me give an example from daily life. Let's say that you have a friend named Joan. You have learned over the years that Joan is honest, hardworking, wise, and friendly. It would be very natural for you to say that you have a lot of faith in Joan—you have confidence in her and you trust her. You know that she consistently does what is right and good and true.

You also have some beliefs about Joan. These beliefs are not based on anything Joan has said to you. You just picked up these beliefs in conversations with others at the office. Based on what you have heard, you believe that Joan was raised in New York, majored in English at college, served in the U.S. Army, and was once a social studies teacher at an intermediate school. You believe she played basketball in college and is taller than you—say, six feet tall. You also think of her as a very gentle, nonviolent person.

Now suppose one day you found out from a mutual friend that Joan was raised in New Mexico, not New York, and she majored in history, not English. Then a few days later, you learned that Joan served in the Peace Corps, not the Army. And a few days after that, another friend told you that Joan didn't teach social studies at an intermediate school but worked with kids in the special education program at an elementary school. She played volleyball in college, not basketball, and the records show that she is not six feet tall but five feet ten inches tall. And you learn that Joan has a few scars from the time she intervened and saved the life of a woman who was being viciously attacked by a man with a knife. Suddenly, a lot of your beliefs about Joan no longer seem to be true.

You may feel a little unsettled, having discovered that you were wrong about some things that you just assumed or surmised from bits of incomplete information. You are going to have to adjust many of your beliefs about Joan, and that's awkward. But the real question is, So what? Joan hasn't changed; only your beliefs about Joan have changed. And the most important thing, your faith in Joan, has not changed at all. You still have a lot of confidence and trust in her. None of the new information changes the fact that she is a good human being, honest, hardworking, wise, and friendly. You still know that she will do what is right and good and true. So your faith in Joan is not affected by a change in your beliefs about her.

CHANGING BELIEFS, UNCHANGING FAITH

We know that our beliefs change as we grow and mature. The simplest way to prove this is to study the same chapter of the Bible every few years. Each time you study it, you will see things that you did not see before. The reason is obvious. The Bible did not change—*you* changed. You grew in understanding, so you have new insights about that Bible chapter. That's why we continually study the Bible, listen to sermons, go on retreats, and try to live our faith in daily life. We want to grow in our understanding.

We need to remember that when we change our beliefs about God, it does not change God. It just means that we have a new—and hopefully deeper—understanding of God.

Habakkuk learned that the God of history, the God who had done battle for his people in the past, could behave differently in the future. So his beliefs about God changed. But his faith remained unshakable.

CHAPTER 7

The Unshakable Faith of Habakkuk

After recalling God's glorious deeds in the past and calling on God to renew those deeds in his day, Habakkuk had a final vision—a vision of the Lord revealing himself in all his might and glory, defeating the Babylonians, and saving his people. The vision included images that recalled God's interventions during the Exodus, his appearance on Mount Sinai, and the conquest of Canaan.

God came from Teman,
    the Holy One from Mount Paran.
His glory covered the heavens
    and his praise filled the earth.

His splendor was like the sunrise;
    rays flashed from his hand,
    where his power was hidden.
Plague went before him;
    pestilence followed his steps.
He stood, and shook the earth;
    he looked, and made the nations tremble.
The ancient mountains crumbled
    and the age-old hills collapsed.
    His ways are eternal.
I saw the tents of Cushan in distress,
    the dwellings of Midian in anguish.[1]

Were you angry with the rivers, O Lord?
    Was your wrath against the streams?
Did you rage against the sea
    when you rode with your horses
    and your victorious chariots?
You uncovered your bow,
    you called for many arrows.
You split the earth with rivers;
    the mountains saw you and writhed.
Torrents of water swept by;
    the deep roared
    and lifted its waves on high. (Hab. 3:3–10)

In Habakkuk's vision, God crushes the leader of the Babylonians and saves the Judeans:

> Sun and moon stood still in the heavens
>> at the glint of your flying arrows,
>> at the lightning of your flashing spear.
> In wrath you strode through the earth
>> and in anger you threshed the nations.
> You came out to deliver your people
>> to save your anointed one.
> You crushed the leader of the land of
> wickedness,
>> you stripped him from head to foot.
> With his own spear you pierced his head
>> when his warriors stormed out to scatter us,
> gloating as though about to devour
>> the wretched who were in hiding.
> You trampled the sea with your horses,
>> churning the great waters. (Hab. 3:11–15)

In response to his complaints, Habakkuk had learned about the destruction and death he and his people would suffer at the hands of the Babylonians. Now, in his final vision, he saw the awesome power of God that would one day be unleashed against the

Babylonians themselves. The future was frightening, and Habakkuk knew fear. It affected him physically.

> I heard and my heart pounded,
>   my lips quivered at the sound;
> Decay crept into my bones,
>   and my legs trembled.
> Yet I will wait patiently for the day of calamity
>   To come on the nation invading us. (Hab. 3:16)

Habakkuk knew that God would be faithful to the covenant he made with his people. The future was fearful, but eventually the day of victory and liberation would come.

REJOICING IN THE LORD

But Habakkuk did more than wait patiently for the day of victory. He was determined to live a life of faith, a life of rejoicing. The final psalm in the book of Habakkuk has been described as "a message of profound hope in a circumstance of profound despair."[2] Habakkuk answered his fears with a song of praise to the Lord.[3]

Though the fig tree does not bud
   and there are no grapes on the vines,
though the olive crop fails
   and the fields produce no food,
though there are no sheep in the pen
   and no cattle in the stalls,
yet I will rejoice in the Lord,
   I will be joyful in God my Savior.
The Sovereign Lord is my strength;
   he makes my feet like the feet of a deer,
   he enables me to go on the heights.[4]
   (Hab. 3:17–19)

To understand the impact of these final verses, we must remember that the kingdom of Judah was agrarian. The economy was based on foodstuffs such as figs, grapes, and olives and livestock like sheep, goats, and cattle. Thus when Habakkuk described a time in which the fig trees do not bud, there are no grapes on the vines, the olive crop fails, the fields produce no food, and there are no sheep or cattle, he is describing complete devastation. The land will be laid waste. There will be nothing to eat. People will starve. Death will be everywhere.[5]

Habakkuk responded to these images of devastation with statements of faith. He knew that even if the land is destroyed by the invading army—even if there is no more food and he is starving—God will still be his Savior and source of strength. God will still give him the energy and confidence to walk on the heights like a deer. Habakkuk knew that he could face the future with the courage and strength that God would give him. With confidence and trust in the Lord, he could face anything. And so Habakkuk rejoiced in his relationship with God, even in the face of devastation and death.

This rejoicing may have been shared with the people of Judah in the temple. The very last words of the book of Habakkuk are "For the director of music. On my stringed instruments." This suggests that the psalm of Habakkuk was used in temple prayers that were chanted with the accompaniment of instruments. The effect of the psalm would have been to rally the Judeans to their God and to inspire their faith.

The faith of Habakkuk can still inspire us today. Whatever happens, we, too, can have unshakable faith. We, too, can rejoice in God our Savior. We, too, can rise to the heights, lifted by our Sovereign Lord.

CHAPTER 8

A Vision for Christians Today

If we were to have a vision today like the vision Habakkuk had 2,600 years ago, what would it be like?

When we look back today, we see God in the Old Testament loving and nurturing his people. We see God's wrath and also God's mercy as he liberates the Hebrews from Egypt, enters into a covenant with them in the desert, and delivers them to a new land. God defends and saves them as they learn what it means to be faithful.

In the book of Habakkuk, we see that God, in God's time, will punish the wicked. We are reminded by the five woes that it is wrong for us as individuals or nations to steal and extort, to seek unjust gains and the ruin of others, to live by bloodshed and crime, to promote debauchery and violence, and to practice idolatry. We are reminded that we should not be the new Babylonians.

When we look back today, we also see what Habakkuk was born too early to see: Jesus Christ. A Christian vision for today builds on the faith of Habakkuk and rises to a new level of hope in Christ. Like Habakkuk, we face death and destruction, but unlike Habakkuk, we know that we have Christ at our side.

Jesus taught us about God and about what God expects of us. Above all, he assured us that God loves us. In fact, God loves us so much that God sent us his only Son to teach us and die for us.

Jesus urged us to repent, "for the kingdom of God is at hand" (Mark 1:15). He explained that the kingdom of God is not like the kingdoms of the earth. Instead, in the Beatitudes, he said that those who will be blessed are the poor in spirit, those who mourn, the meek, those who hunger and thirst for righteousness, the merciful, the pure in heart, the peacemakers, and those who are persecuted because of righteousness (Matt. 5:3–12). Unless we become like children, we will not enter the kingdom of heaven (Matt. 18:3).

Jesus taught us to ask for what we need because our Father loves us and will respond (Matt. 7:7–11). Jesus taught us that when we have faith, we can trust God and not worry so much (Matt. 6:25–33).[1]

When we live a life of faith, we know that many good things will happen, not solely because of our own efforts but also because of God's grace. In the parable of the growing seed, Jesus said:

> This is what the kingdom of God is like. A man scatters seed on the ground. Night and day, whether he sleeps or gets up, the seed sprouts and grows, though he does not know how. All by itself the soil produces grain—first the stalk, then the head, then the full kernel in the head. As soon as the grain is ripe, he puts the sickle to it, because the harvest has come. (Mark 4:26–29)

We need to find good soil and scatter the seed. We need to harvest the crop when it is grown. But the rest is God's doing.

Jesus taught us how to live. He taught us to love God with all our heart and soul and mind. He taught us to love our neighbors as ourselves (Matt. 22:37–40). He taught us to love our enemies (Matt. 5:43–48).

This kind of love is described as *agape*, the love of Christians for others that corresponds to God's unconditional love for all humankind.

Jesus described his disciples as being *in* the world, not *of* the world (John 17:14–15). In the parable of the Good Samaritan, he taught us to take care of others (Luke 10:30–35). In the parable of the sheep and the goats, he said that those who will live with him in eternity will be those who feed the hungry, give drink to the thirsty, offer hospitality to strangers, clothe the naked, look after the sick, and visit prisoners (Matt. 25:31–46). He taught us that we are not measured by the abundance of our possessions (Luke 12:15). He urged us to store up our treasures in heaven, not on earth (Matt. 6:19–21). He affirmed the Golden Rule: "So in everything, do to others what you would have them do to you, for this sums up the Law and the Prophets" (Matt. 7:12).

Jesus knew that we would need guidance and courage to live the way he taught us to live. He told his disciples that they would receive power when the Holy Spirit came upon them (Acts 1:8). The Holy Spirit descended on the apostles as they were gathered together on Pentecost. This was a new kind of incarnation, the incarnation of God in a new church, a church called to live the way Jesus taught us to live, a church strengthened by the inspiration of the Holy Spirit.

Today, we have faith and confidence in a triune God—the Father who created the universe and nurtured his people, the Son who taught us and died for us, and the Holy Spirit who is among us, guiding and encouraging us. We have the strongest possible foundation for unshakable faith. And we know how God wants us to live.

We do not know what our future holds. We can see despair and death from violence, injustice, starvation, disease, and environmental destruction. But as Christians, we can envision the day when we will be at peace with ourselves and others. We can envision the day when we will love each other and help each other and respect each other as children of God. We can envision the day when we will be in harmony with the natural world God created for us. We can envision the day when justice will reign and people will no longer be oppressed. We can envision the day when hunger and disease will no longer plague hundreds of millions of people. We can envision the day described in Habakkuk's vision, the day when "the earth will be filled with the knowledge of the glory of the Lord, as the waters cover the sea" (Hab. 2:14).

We must live the way Jesus taught us to live, and we must take action. There will be problems; there will be days when the obstacles will seem overwhelming. But if we want to make our vision a reality, we must move forward in faith. No matter how difficult it becomes, we must *have faith anyway.*

 CHAPTER 9

Your Own Vision: An Invitation

I believe that God is still speaking to us. If we have faith and listen, we will hear him. We may have our own visions of a conversation with God. They may not be like the vision of Habakkuk, but they may be visions that inspire us and strengthen our faith and commitment to fulfill God's purposes.

I encourage you to study the book of Habakkuk and pray on what it means in our time. I invite you to be open to receiving your own vision.

I studied and prayed on the book of Habakkuk for months. Then one morning, as I walked to the YMCA to work out, words began coming to me. As I exercised, the words kept coming, rhythmically, rapidly, in large blocks of dialogue. The dialogue was between a Christian and God. There was a sense of urgency in the words. I hurried back to my office, sat down at my computer, and began typing furiously. Fortunately, the words were still there. The words were poignant, direct, and demanding, but there was also a kind of purity, clarity, and joy in them that touched me deeply. Over the next few days, more words came at different times, mostly in short phrases, which I wrote down on any piece of paper that was handy— a sales receipt, a paper towel, a sheet of notebook paper. I did my best to organize the words into a meaningful sequence. Writing the dialogue was one of the most exciting experiences of my life.

I do not claim to have had a conversation with God. I had a vision that consisted of words—separate sections of a dialogue between a Christian and God that I arranged into a single conversation. Here is that conversation:

Lord?

I am here.

Lord, I look out at the world, and I feel a lot of anguish.

I am listening.

Lord, our world is a mess. People are at war. People are dying of hunger and thirst. People are dying of diseases. The atmosphere is warming, and we are headed for an environmental disaster. And there are more than enough nuclear warheads to kill us all, many times over.

Yes, you have made quite a mess of the world I created for you.

And it is getting worse.

Yes, just as in the time of Habakkuk, it will get worse before it gets better.

There is so much evil and corruption. It seems to be everywhere—in government, in business, in social institutions.

Yes, just as in the time of Habakkuk, there is much evil and corruption.

Lord, this is your world. You created it. And we are your people. We need your help. We need you to step in. What are you doing to make things better?

I am allowing you the freedom of will to discover the most important thing you need to learn.

What is that?

That you are all my children.

Why is it so important to learn that?

You will learn it or you will die. You will not survive unless you come together.

Come together?

The problems you must solve cannot be solved by any one nation, religion, ethnic group, or economy. You must come together. All of you.

But we have different cultures and languages.

Come together.

We have different religions.

Come together.

We suffer from ancient animosities.

Come together.

We are rich and poor. There are a lot of economic problems.

Come together.

We don't all look the same either.

Come together.

You know we've never really done anything on a worldwide basis before.

Come together.

We don't have the knowledge.

You know how to produce food, but you do not share your surplus with others, so people starve. You have discovered cures for diseases, but you do not share those cures with others, so people die. You have developed technology that makes it easier to communicate than ever before, but you do not try to understand each other. You have knowledge. You do not have love.

You're asking us to really grow spiritually—to really change.

Yes.

This is going to take a major breakthrough.

I sent you a major breakthrough. I sent you my Son.

Yes, Lord, you did. So how do we start?

Jesus told you how to start.

You must be referring to the part about loving people.

Yes.

Loving everybody.

Yes.

Did Jesus really mean we should love our enemies?

Yes.

Right.

He taught you to feed the hungry, give drink to the thirsty, welcome strangers, clothe the naked, look after the sick, and visit those in prison.

Right.

He taught you to not store up treasures on earth but in heaven.

Right.

He taught you to be peacemakers.

Right. But things won't change until we have a lot more believers.

There are already enough people who believe in Christ. There are not enough people who follow Jesus.

Yes. I understand. We need to both worship Christ and follow Jesus.

If you do, the children of God will come together.

When you say "come together," do you mean we must all become Christians?

No. Not all will believe. But if you love others as I love you, you can all come together.

Do we have to agree on everything?

No. You don't have to agree on everything to come together. Love is deeper than agreement or approval.

Is our future going to be like the Babylonian captivity that followed the vision of Habakkuk?

No. Your task is different from the task of the people of Judah during the Babylonian captivity.

How is it different?

The Judeans in the Babylonian captivity could survive only by clinging to each other. You can survive only by reaching out to others, beyond yourselves.

This is pretty new.

No, this is very old. I shared the vision with Isaiah. Remember the mountain of the Lord. All nations will stream to it. I will settle disputes for many peoples. They will beat their swords into plowshares and their spears into pruning hooks. Nation will not take up sword against nation, nor will they train for war anymore.

We are living in turbulent times. I have a few questions about that. Are all the wars and diseases and poverty that we see today part of the End Times?

No, they are part of your times.

When will the Second Coming occur?

When the earth is filled with the knowledge of the glory of the Lord, as the waters cover the sea.

Who is the Anti-Christ?

Anyone who walks the land with hate and violence in his heart is an anti-Christ.

Who will live in the New Jerusalem?

The New Jerusalem is for all my children.

But not all believe in Christ.

When they see Christ reigning in the New Jerusalem, they will understand who Christ is, and they will believe.

So the time has come to go out to all the nations, loving and helping everybody.

Yes.

The time has come to remind everyone that we are all God's children.

Yes.

That's pretty dramatic.

Yes. People will notice. Attitudes will change.

We may become discouraged.

The Holy Spirit will be with you.

We may be crucified.

Christ will be with you.

We may lose the way.

I will be with you. I love you—all of you.

I praise you, Lord.

Remember, the righteous will live by his faith.

I will remember, Lord.

Then you will go out in joy
  and be led forth in peace;
The mountains and hills
  will burst into song before you,
and all the trees of the field
  will clap their hands.
Instead of the thornbush will grow the pine tree,
  and instead of briers the myrtle will grow.
This will be for the Lord's renown,
  for an everlasting sign,
which will not be destroyed.

Thank you, Lord. Thank you!

Now go in peace, and change the world.

READER'S GUIDE
FOR REFLECTION AND STUDY

The purpose of the Reader's Guide is to help you strengthen your own faith. The questions are designed for both personal reflection and group discussion. Some questions focus on the text, while others provide quotations from other sources that can deepen your understanding of the text.

CHAPTER ONE: THE PROPHET WHO CONFRONTED GOD

1. According to the *Random House Webster's Unabridged Dictionary*, a prophet is "a person chosen to speak for God and to guide the people of Israel" (p. 1550). David Freedman's *Anchor Bible Dictionary* says:

> Divine inspiration was what made a person a
> prophet, and what caused the prophet to speak out,

and what made others listen to the prophet. . . .
The prophet is the one who can speak in the name
of God. . . . Many of the early prophets speak only
to individuals, especially kings or other officials,
while other, later prophets address large groups
of people—rhetorically, the whole nation or an
entire city. . . . They spoke in poetry, and some
of the poetry that the prophets created is virtually
unmatched in world literature. . . . The first demand
of the prophets was that the people worship only
Yahweh. . . . The right worship of God requires of
a person the right treatment of one's fellow human
beings. The prophets do not tolerate worship of
God that is not linked to proper behavior toward
one's neighbor. (pp. 482–484)

Here is a list of the prophets, in the order in which
their books appear in the Old Testament: Isaiah,
Jeremiah, Ezekiel, Daniel, Hosea, Joel, Amos, Obadiah,
Jonah, Micah, Nahum, Habakkuk, Zephaniah, Haggai,
Zechariah, Malachi. Which of them spoke to kings or
other officials, and which addressed larger groups? How
did that affect the way they delivered their messages?
Do you see any patterns? Give some examples of prophets demanding that members of their audience behave
properly toward their neighbors.

2.   Many people think of the prophets as people who "prophesied" by foretelling the future. Richard Rohr and Joseph Martos, in *The Great Themes of Scripture: The Old Testament*, said this about the prophets:

> The prophet is not so much one who sees into the future as one who sees clearly in the present. He is not so much a man of foresight as a man of insight. Such a person right now, in the present, listens to the Lord and speaks the word he or she hears. The prophet hears what is real, and he speaks it to the world. . . . The prophets were the social conscience of Israel, just as prophets in our own day are people of great conscience. . . . They look into the present situation to see which patterns can be detected in the world around them: Is it the pattern of salvation, which leads to life, or is it the pattern of sin, which leads to death? If their prophetic insight tells them that it is the latter, they proclaim: "This is not the way of God! You're going in the wrong direction!". . . They cannot tell the future, but they can tell the future will be bad unless the people change their ways. (pp. 64–66)

Was Habakkuk a man of insight, foresight, or both? Was he a "social conscience" of Israel? As a result of his vision, could he tell the future?

3. Abraham Heschel, in *The Prophets,* notes that "the prophet's words are outbursts of violent emotions. . . . The prophet is a man who feels fiercely" (p. 5). Heschel explains:

> To us a single act of injustice—cheating in business, exploitation of the poor—is slight; to the prophets, a disaster. To us injustice is injurious to the welfare of the people; to the prophets it is a deathblow to existence: to us, an episode; to them, a catastrophe, a threat to the world. Their breathless impatience with injustice may strike us as hysteria. We ourselves witness continually acts of injustice, manifestations of hypocrisy, falsehood, outrage, misery, but we rarely grow indignant or overly excited. . . . Our eyes are witness to the callousness and cruelty of man, but our heart tries to obliterate the memories, to calm the nerves, and to silence our conscience. (pp. 4–5)

Did Habakkuk feel fiercely? Did acts of injustice strike him as a disaster? Do you think small injustices and cruelties open the gates to larger ones? Do we still need to hear the voices of the prophets?

4. David Baker, in *Nahum, Habakkuk, Zephaniah*, writes:

> The role of a prophet was to bring the nation and its leaders back to obedience to the covenant which God had made with his people at Sinai. If covenant obligations were neglected or abandoned, the prophet, often at some personal peril, would confront the wrongdoers and demand repentance in the name of Yahweh. (p. 47)

What was different about the role of Habakkuk compared with other prophets?

5. David Zucker, in *Israel's Prophets*, says that "while internal political developments concerned the prophets, they were likewise aware of the wider geopolitical configurations of their day" (p. 23). They knew about other nations—their kings, armies, and living conditions, as well as trade and political alliances between nations. What wider geopolitical configurations would a prophet be aware of today?

6. Can you name any prophets in recent history?

CHAPTER TWO: THE ANGUISH OF HABAKKUK

1. Do you see parallels between the violence, wickedness, and injustice that Habakkuk faced and the problems that we face throughout the world today?

2. Have you ever been angry with God? If so, what were you angry about?

3. The argument about evil is an ancient one. People say that if God is both good and omnipotent, God would stop all evil from occurring. Since God has not stopped all evil, they conclude that God is not good or God is not omnipotent or God is neither. Others counter by saying that God is good and omnipotent, but God has created natural laws that govern the universe, and God has given us free will to make our own decisions. Evil therefore exists because of natural events like fires, floods, hurricanes, and earthquakes or because human beings use their freedom to behave in evil ways. What do you think? Why do you think evil exists?

4. When you have thought of the evil in the world or of the bad things that have happened to you and

those close to you, have you tried to see God in all the mess? Has your faith been affected? What insights have you had? Where did you find help for living by faith even in very hard times?

5. Peter Craigie, in *Twelve Prophets*, notes that the value of the book of Habakkuk to the continuing community of faith is that "it raises openly the kinds of questions that any thinking and believing person ought to ask" (p. 84). What questions do you want to ask God?

6. In *The NIV Application Commentary*, James Bruckner writes:

> Questions and lament are part of a believer's burden, and honest dialogue with God is a necessary form of relationship with him. . . . Lamentation and questioning are God's gift to the believer. They provide a pathway of honest faith and faithful conversation with him in horrible times. . . . Those who long for the kingdom of God with its peace, love, and goodness may find hope on the pathway of lament and faithful protest. (pp. 214–215)

Have lamentation and questioning been part of your faith and conversation with God? If so, in what ways?

7. O. Palmer Robertson, in *The Books of Nahum, Habakkuk, and Zephaniah,* emphasizes the fact that God did not rebuke Habakkuk for his complaints, even though Habakkuk expected to be rebuked. Robertson says, "The Lord himself is fully in sympathy with the prophet's agony over the suffering righteous ones. Although having larger concerns as well, the Lord knows and sympathizes with these who have been surrounded by the wicked" (p. 141). How do you sense God's sympathy when you are angry or confused about what God is doing? What helps you?

CHAPTER THREE: IN GOD'S TIME, NOT OUR TIME

1. Peter Craigie, in Twelve Prophets, writes:

> God's apparent inaction in response to evil was a source of difficulty for the prophet [Habakkuk], but he had made the mistake of measuring God on the human scale of time. He had thought that God does not act, but he was coming to realize that God had simply not acted yet. He knew that God ought to act in response to evil, and in this he was correct; he thought he knew *when* God ought to act, and in this

he was wrong. . . . [H]uman beings do not have either the knowledge or wisdom to know *when* God should act. . . . The apparent lack of divine action, which may cause faith to falter, is in reality only our inability to perceive the timing of divine action. (pp. 92–93)

Can you think of a situation in your own life when you thought that God would not act but later saw that God had simply *not acted yet*?

2.   What does "in God's time" mean to you?

3.   Are you good at waiting for God's time, or do you really want him to follow your personal timetable?

4.   How does God speak to you in your daily life? Have you found ways to make time to hear God when God speaks to you? If not, what is preventing you from doing so?

5.   Habakkuk said, "I will stand at my watch and station myself on the ramparts; I will look to see what he will say to me, and what answer I am to give to this complaint" (Hab. 2:1). Give some examples of how you "stand and watch." What have you discovered?

CHAPTER FOUR: THE LESSONS
OF THE FIVE WOES

1. God's answer to Habakkuk's second complaint began by describing someone who is "puffed up." What does it mean to be "puffed up"? How would that have been defined in Habakkuk's society, and how would we define it today in ours?

2. Review the deeds described in each of the five woes. Cite some examples of that behavior in our world today.

3. Habakkuk 2:14 says, "For the earth will be filled with the knowledge of the glory of the Lord, as the waters cover the sea." The verse is based on an earlier verse in Isaiah 11:6–9 that envisions a peaceful kingdom. James Bruckner, in *The NIV Application Commentary*, states that the phrase "the earth will be filled with the knowledge of the glory of the Lord, as the waters cover the sea" expresses God's ultimate purpose in the world. It is a declaration that refers to "God's intention to bless all the nations of the world through Israel by bringing the whole creation back to the Creator through Israel's history" (p. 231).

What do you think the world would be like today if it was "filled with the knowledge of the glory of the Lord, as the waters cover the sea"?

4. The Preface describes "deep happiness" as the kind of happiness that touches the spirit and connects with the soul. Have you experienced that kind of happiness? When? What was it like?

CHAPTER FIVE: LIVING BY FAITH

1. The second phrase in Habakkuk 2:4 (referred to as Hab. 2:4b), has been translated in a variety of ways. Here are a few of the available translations:

> *New International Version* (used in this text): "the righteous will live by his faith."
> *New American Bible:* "the just man, because of his faith, shall live."
> *New Revised Standard Version:* "the righteous live by their faith."
> *King James Version:* "the just shall live by his faith."
> *Jewish Publication Society:* "the righteous man is rewarded with life for his fidelity."

The Message: "the person in right standing before God through loyal and steady believing is fully alive, *really alive.*"

Discuss the different translations. Do you have a preference? If so, why? If not, why not?

2. What do "righteous" and "just" mean to you? Do they mean moral, proper, virtuous, principled, upright, holy, or some combination of these concepts—or something else?

3. What does "faith" mean to you? What are the sources of your personal faith? What does it mean to live by your faith?

4. As noted in question 1, Eugene Peterson, in *The Message*, translated Habakkuk 2:4b as "the person in right standing before God through loyal and steady believing is fully alive, *really* alive" (p. 1695). How does your faith help you to be fully alive, *really* alive?

5. James Bruckner, in *The NIV Application Commentary*, states that the phrase "the righteous will live by his faith" means that "those who want to live

in right relationship with God and his people will live by their trust in the promises of the Lord" (p. 227). Do you trust in the promises of the Lord? What promises has God made to us?

6. Habakkuk 2:4 says, "See, he is puffed up; his desires are not upright—but the righteous will live by his faith." O. Palmer Robertson, in *The Books of Nahum, Habakkuk, and Zephaniah*, highlights the contrast between Habakkuk 2:4a and 2:4b. He writes:

> The message that a person shall "live by faith" underscores the fact that life is a gift, received gratefully from the Lord's hand. Standing in sharpest contradiction to the "proud" who are "not upright" in themselves and therefore must die, the one who trusts God's grace for his existence every moment shall live. He shall survive the devastations of God's judgment. (p. 178)

What does it mean to trust God's grace for your existence every moment?

7. Lawrence Boadt, in *Reading the Old Testament*, says that the message God sends to Habakkuk is that "the righteous who believe will live, the wicked will

not succeed" (p. 358). Do you agree? What does this message mean to you? If it seems to contradict what you see in the world around you, what do you make of that?

8. Where do you see God in your daily life?

9. Have you experienced the healing power of Christ through your faith?

10. The book of Hebrews describes the faith of Abel, Enoch, Noah, Abraham, Isaac, Jacob, Joseph, and Moses. Faith is "what the ancients were commended for" (Heb. 11:2). Richard Rohr and Joseph Martos, in *The Great Themes of Scripture: Old Testament*, point out that the eleventh chapter of the Epistle to the Hebrews "looks at the whole development of the Old Testament as a history of faith, a history of people hoping for what they could not yet see but following confidently the lead of the Lord in the assurance that what they were hoping for would eventually happen" (p. 109). Was that faith fulfilled? If so, how?

11. Habakkuk 2:4b ("the righteous will live by his faith") has been important to both Jews and

Christians for centuries. The verse has been described by Jewish rabbis as "the kernel of Judaism" (Wigoder, p. 299). Talmudic Rabbi Simlai cited it as a summary of all 613 commandments of the Torah (*Encyclopedia Judaica*, p. 1017). As noted in Chapter Five, Paul quoted it in Romans 1:17 and Galatians 3:11, giving it "a prominent place in his own teaching on faith" (Brown, Fitzmyer, and Murphy, p. 261). It can also be found at Hebrews 10:38. These New Testament passages provided a scriptural basis for the doctrine of "justification by faith" that was a focal point for Martin Luther during the Reformation (Freedman, vol. 3, p. 5).

Why do you think Habakkuk 2:4b has been so important to Jews and Christians? What was it in Habakkuk's vision that resonated with them? Why was this so important to them in their historical and religious contexts?

CHAPTER SIX: FAITH VERSUS BELIEFS

1. Richard Rohr and Joseph Martos, in *The Great Themes of Scripture: Old Testament,* assert that there are four stages or levels in the journey of faith: (1) people

start to experience the reality of God and his love; (2) people begin to respond to God's love but think that God's love is dependent on their response; (3) people begin to see God's love as unlimited and unconditional; and (4) people make the breakthrough and see that God's grace and love are incarnate in human lives and interactions (pp. 112–113). Where do you think you are in your faith journey? How can you move forward?

2.   Is the description of the difference between "faith" and "beliefs" that is made in this chapter helpful to you? If so, why? If not, why not?

3.   What could cause our beliefs about God to change through the years?

4.   Which of your beliefs have changed even while your faith has remained strong?

5.   Have any of your beliefs changed and weakened your faith? If so, how did you strengthen your faith again?

6.   Which of your beliefs have stayed the same?

CHAPTER SEVEN: THE UNSHAKABLE FAITH OF HABAKKUK

1. O. Palmer Robertson, in *The Books of Nahum, Habakkuk, and Zephaniah*, writes:

> The underlying theme of the book [of Habakkuk] may be summarized as follows: *A matured faith trusts humbly but persistently in God's design for establishing righteousness in the earth.* Remarkably, the reader is allowed the unique privilege of witnessing the progress of the prophet himself in submitting to a new concept of the Lord's purposes among Israel and the nations. The idea of growth or maturing faith is essential to appreciating the genius of this prophecy. Trust in the purposes of the Lord despite confusing perceptions of precisely what he is doing lies at the center of the thought of Habakkuk. Broader intentions of the Lord come to the fore as the prophet wrestles with progressive disclosures. (p. 136)

Can you track the stages of growth in Habakkuk's faith from the first chapter to the third chapter?

2. Habakkuk's confidence in God was based on his relationship with God and on his knowledge of God's

past deeds as a powerful warrior and merciful Lord. Where does your confidence in God come from?

3. Are there things that God has done in the past that constitute a foundation for your own faith?

4. Compare Job and Habakkuk. Job suffered and argued with the Lord but never lost his faith. Habakkuk confronted the Lord, learned about the coming destruction, and still had faith. But Habakkuk did more than accept the coming destruction. What else did he do?

5. In his *Introduction to the Old Testament*, Walter Brueggemann says that the book of Habakkuk "consists in already existing liturgical pieces that are woven together here in a fresh way: dialogue and complaint and responding oracle, "alas" oracles, and theophanic resolution in a hymnic voice" (p. 243). What would have been the impact on the people of Judah in Habakkuk's day when he shared a new vision from God that incorporated earlier scriptures?

6. Do you rejoice in your relationship with God, even when times are tough and the future is uncertain?

7. Write your own version of Habakkuk 3:17–19, describing current or potential problems in your own life. For example, "Though my son becomes sick and my car breaks down; though I am fired from my job and my bank account goes dry, . . ."

CHAPTER EIGHT: A VISION FOR CHRISTIANS TODAY

1. What do we know about God from the Old Testament, especially the book of Habakkuk?

2. What assurances about God do we have from Jesus?

3. How does the kingdom of God that is described by Jesus differ from the kingdoms of this world?

4. Does your faith help you worry less? (Matt. 6:25–34)

5. What did Jesus teach us about how we should live?

6. Is it hard to live the way Jesus taught us to live? Why or why not? Share your own personal experiences.

7. What do you think are the most important elements in a Christian vision of the future?

CHAPTER NINE: YOUR OWN VISION:
AN INVITATION

1. In my vision of a conversation with God, God made reference to Isaiah 2:1–4 and 55:12–13, Habakkuk 2:4 and 2:14, and Matthew 5:9, 6:19–20, and 25:34–36. Can you identify these verses in the conversation?

2. How do you see the situation in the world today? Share your views regarding politics and government, society and culture, economics and the workplace, the natural environment, and spirituality and religion.

3. How do you think God is using the present situation to bring about his kingdom?

4. What can you do to respond to God and help fulfill God's purposes? What can your church do? What can your community do?

5. Through study and prayer, can you discern your own vision of a conversation with God about the issues that we face in our world today? If so, write it down and share it with others.

NOTES

CHAPTER ONE: THE PROPHET WHO CONFRONTED GOD

1 See Bruckner, *The NIV Application Commentary*, p. 199; International Bible Society, *NIV Archeological Study Bible*, p. 1506; and Baker, *Nahum, Habakkuk, Zephaniah*, p. 43.

2 Bruckner, p. 202; Baker, p. 45; Craigie, *Twelve Prophets*, vol. 2, p. 77.

3 All biblical quotations are from the New International Version (NIV) unless otherwise indicated. In the NIV, the word translated as *oracle* means "burden." See Bruckner, p. 200, and O. Palmer Robertson, *The Books of Nahum, Habakkuk, and Zephaniah*, p. 135.

4 See Boadt, *Reading the Old Testament*, p. 459, and Bright, *A History of Israel*, pp. 316–327. The events of this period, from the fall of the northern kingdom of Israel through the fall of Judah, are found in the Bible at 2 Kings:17–25.

5 Bury, Cook, and Adcock, *The Cambridge Ancient History*, p. 399.

6 Bright, pp. 327–330. Bright refers to the year 587 B.C.; some historians place the date of the fall of Jerusalem a year later, in 586. See, for example, Orlinsky, *Ancient Israel*, p. 97, and Bury, Cook, and Adcock, p. 402.

7 Von Rad, *The Message of the Prophets*, p. 158; Baker, p. 44. Scholars offer various estimates of the period in which the book of Habakkuk was written. Craigie, p. 77, estimates that the book of Habakkuk was written between 610 and 605 B.C., while Bruckner, p. 202, asserts that "Habakkuk prophesied the fall of Judah to Babylon in the year of the Babylonians' victory over the Egyptians at Carchemish in northern Syria (605 B.C.)." Andersen suggests that Habakkuk was written during the period between 605 (the Battle of Carchemish) and 575 B.C. See Andersen, *Habakkuk*, p. 27. Roberts, in *Nahum, Habakkuk, and Zephaniah*, p. 83, argues that the individual oracles in the book of Habakkuk were given at widely separated times, some dating before 605 and others after 597 B.C.. Childs, in *Introduction to the Old Testament as Scripture*, p. 452, says that the book of Habakkuk appears to reflect oracles written during several periods—a time before the Babylonian invasion, a period subsequent to the first exile in 597 B.C., and the second exile in 587 B.C.

CHAPTER THREE: IN GOD'S TIME, NOT OUR TIME

1 Scholars do not agree regarding the revelation that is referred to in Hab. 2:2–3 (the revelation that God told

Habakkuk to wait for in his second answer). Heschel, in *The Prophets*, says, "Habakkuk's vision remains unknown to us. Its content is not put into words. It clearly was a vision of redemption at the end of days. . . . It is an answer, not in terms of thought, but in terms of events" (p. 182). Robertson provides a different view, which is that the vision referred to in Hab. 2:2–3 is found immediately afterward in Hab. 2:4–5, the passage that describes the person who is puffed up, and includes the phrase "the righteous will live by his faith" (p. 174). A third view is held by Roberts, who writes that the revelation referred to in Hab. 2:2–3 is finally recorded in Hab. 3:3–15, the vision of the glory of the Lord. Roberts says, "This vision of Yahweh's coming intervention against the powers of chaos, embodied at the moment in the Babylonians, makes a tremendous impression on the prophet, and he confesses his willingness to wait patiently for God to resolve the problem of injustice that the prophet had struggled with for so long" (p. 81).

CHAPTER FOUR: THE LESSONS OF THE FIVE WOES

1 See, for example, Gowan, *The Triumph of Faith in Habakkuk*, pp. 57–58.

2 See Brueggemann, *An Introduction to the Old Testament*, p. 242; Bruckner, p. 243; and Gowan, p. 53.

3　Baker, pp. 62–68, refers to these as taunting woes against the pillager, the plotter, the promoter of violence, the debaucher, and the pagan idolator.

4　Baker, p. 62.

5　One of the best-known verses in Habakkuk is 2:20: "But the Lord is in his holy temple; let all the earth be silent before him." This verse contrasts the living Lord with Babylonian idols. The Babylonians created idols of wood and metal and then expected those inanimate objects to "speak to them" and give them guidance. When the idols did not respond, the Babylonians would shout at them to awaken them. Baker, pp. 67–68, says:

> The true source of revelation . . . is present where he has always been, *in his holy temple*. . . . Yahweh is approached in silence, a fitting response to his holiness and majesty, and a token of one's respect for his being—dependency upon his grace and submission to his will. . . . This silence is requested not only of Judah but of *all the earth*, who will ultimately acknowledge God as the true giver of knowledge. . . . This contrasts with the frenetic activity of man to create "speaking" gods, and the tumultuous cries of worshippers to make dumb idols respond. Lifeless idols approached in clamour are silent, while the living God, approached in silence and reverence, speaks.

CHAPTER FIVE: LIVING BY FAITH

1 Baker, p. 48.

2 *Random House Webster's Unabridged Dictionary*, p. 693.

3 Keith, *Jesus Did It Anyway*, pp. 11–27.

4 See also the story of the Canaanite woman at Matthew 15:21–28 and the story of the centurion at Matthew 8:5–13 and Luke 7:1–10.

5 See also Mark 11:22.

6 See also 1 Corinthians 4:16–18.

CHAPTER SIX: FAITH VERSUS BELIEFS

1 See, for example, Haight, *Dynamics of Theology*, pp. 26–29.

2 See, for example, Rhodes, *The Complete Guide to Christian Denominations*, pp. 58, 110, 116, and 177.

CHAPTER SEVEN: THE UNSHAKABLE FAITH OF HABAKKUK

1 "Teman" and "Mount Paran," both located south of Judah, may refer to the boundaries of the desert through which God led the Israelites to the Promised Land. "Cushan" and "Midian" might refer to two nomadic tribes associated with

the Sinai peninsula. "Cushan" might also refer to Ethiopia. See Robertson, pp. 222, 227–229.

2 Brueggemann, p. 244.

3 The third chapter of Habakkuk—the prayer or psalm—has had a significant impact on both Jewish and Christian faith communities. It is understood by the Jewish community as "a description of the revelation at Sinai and is read as the Haphtarah section for the second day of the Festival of Shavuot, which commemorates the revelation of the Torah at Sinai" (Wigoder, *The Encyclopedia of Judaism*, p. 299). The third chapter of Habakkuk is also included in the liturgy of Christian denominations.

4 The last two verses, Habakkuk 3:18–19, echo other verses in the Old Testament. See, for example, Deuteronomy 32:13; 2 Samuel 22:34; Psalms 18:33, 46:1, and 97:12; and Isaiah 61:10.

5 As these final verses demonstrate, Habakkuk's vision included images and scriptural passages that were common in his day. The references to the fig tree, vines, the olive crop, fields, sheep, and cattle are similar to those found in the Old Testament books of Joel and Jeremiah. Joel may have been written in the ninth century B.C., two hundred years before Habakkuk, and Jeremiah is thought to have been a contemporary of Habakkuk. We find these words at Joel 1:10: "The fields are ruined, the ground is dried up, the grain is destroyed, the new wine is dried up, the oil fails." Joel 1:12 says, "The vine is dried up and the fig tree is withered."

Jeremiah spoke of the destructive invasion of the army of a distant nation. The Lord in Jeremiah 5:17 said, "They will devour your harvests and food, devour your sons and daughters; they will devour your flocks and herds, devour your vines and fig trees."

CHAPTER EIGHT: A VISION FOR CHRISTIANS TODAY

1   See also Luke 12:22–34.

 REFERENCES

Andersen, Francis I. *Habakkuk: A New Translation with Introduction and Commentary*. New York: Anchor/Doubleday, 2001.

Baker, David W. *Nahum, Habakkuk, Zephaniah: An Introduction and Commentary* (Tyndale Old Testament Commentaries). Leicester, England: Intervarsity Press, 1988.

Boadt, Lawrence. *Reading the Old Testament: An Introduction*. New York: Paulist Press, 1984.

Bright, John. *A History of Israel* (4th ed.). Louisville, Ky.: Westminster/John Knox, 2000.

Brown, Raymond E., Joseph A. Fitzmyer, and Roland E. Murphy (eds.). *The New Jerome Biblical Commentary*. Upper Saddle River, N.J.: Prentice Hall, 1990.

Bruckner, James. *The NIV Application Commentary: Jonah, Nahum, Habakkuk, Zephaniah*. Grand Rapids, Mich.: Zondervan, 2004.

Brueggemann, Walter. *An Introduction to the Old Testament*. Louisville, Ky.: Westminster/John Knox, 2003.

Bury, J. B., S. A. Cook, and F. E. Adcock (eds.). *The Cambridge Ancient History*. London: Cambridge University Press, 1925.

Childs, Brevard S. *Introduction to the Old Testament as Scripture*. Philadelphia: Fortress Press, 1979.

Craigie, Peter C. *Twelve Prophets, Vol. 2: Micah, Nahum, Habakkuk, Zephaniah, Haggai, Zechariah, and Malachi*. London: Westminster/John Knox, 1985.

Encyclopedia Judaica. New York: Macmillan, 1971.

Freedman, David N. (ed.). *The Anchor Bible Dictionary*. New York: Doubleday, 1992.

Gowan, Donald E. *The Triumph of Faith in Habakkuk*. Atlanta: John Knox Press, 1976.

Haight, Roger. *Dynamics of Theology*. Maryknoll, N.Y.: Orbis Books, 2001.

Heschel, Abraham J. *The Prophets*. New York: HarperPerennial Modern Classics, 2001. (Originally published 1962)

International Bible Society. *NIV Archeological Study Bible*. Grand Rapids, Mich.: Zondervan, 2005.

Keith, Kent M. *Jesus Did It Anyway: The Paradoxical Commandments for Christians*. New York: Putnam, 2005.

Orlinsky, Harry M. *Ancient Israel*. Ithaca, N.Y.: Cornell University Press, 1960.

Peterson, Eugene H. *The Message: The Bible in Contemporary Language*. Colorado Springs, Colo.: NavPress, 2002.

Random House Webster's Unabridged Dictionary (2nd ed.). New York: Random House, 2001.

Rhodes, Ron. *The Complete Guide to Christian Denominations*. Eugene, Ore.: Harvest House, 2005.

Roberts, J.J.M. *Nahum, Habakkuk, and Zephaniah*. Louisville, Ky.: Westminster/John Knox, 1991.

Robertson, O. Palmer. *The Books of Nahum, Habakkuk, and Zephaniah* (New International Commentary on the Old Testament). Grand Rapids, Mich.: Eerdmans, 1990.

Rohr, Richard, and Joseph Martos. *The Great Themes of Scripture: The Old Testament*. (Cincinnati: Saint Anthony Messenger Press, 1988.

Von Rad, Gerhard. *The Message of the Prophets*. San Francisco: HarperOne, 1962, 1965.

Wigoder, Geoffrey (ed.). *The Encyclopedia of Judaism*. New York: Macmillan, 1989.

Zucker, David J. *Israel's Prophets: An Introduction for Christians and Jews*. New York: Paulist Press, 1994.

ACKNOWLEDGMENTS

I am grateful for the insights and profound faith of my many friends who commented on the manuscript. My heartfelt thanks to Dr. David Anderson; Don Anderson; Rev. Don Asman; Rev. John Bolin, S.M.; Jerry Glashagel; Rev. Dan Hatch; Rev. John Heidel; Nobue Izutsu; Keith Johnston; Dr. Wally Johnston; Rev. William Kaina; Elizabeth Keith; Evelyn Keith; Kristina Keith; Greg Kemp; Linda Kramer; Rev. Nelson Kwon; Rev. Scott Lewis, S.J.; Rabbi Avi Magid; Brian Melzack; Dr. Fran Newman; Dr. Sheryl Nojima; Mary Tikalsky; Jean Varney; Charlotte Walters; Jana Wolff; and Dr. Takeshi Yoshihara.

My special thanks to Rev. Don Asman for introducing me to Habakkuk and to Dr. David Anderson, Dr. David Coleman, Dr. Regina Pfeiffer, Dean Frank McGinnis, and Dr. Peter Steiger of the religion faculty at Chaminade University for teaching me my first courses in theology.

My wife, Elizabeth Keith, not only made the connection with the eleventh Paradoxical Commandment and commented on the manuscript but also provided ongoing support and encouragement. My agents, Roger Jellinek and Eden-Lee Murray, provided valuable advice at every stage in the development of the book. At Jossey-Bass, I am grateful for the important insights of my editor, Sheryl Fullerton, and the professionalism of the members of the entire production team: Alison Knowles, Robin Lloyd, Michael Cook, Jennifer Wenzel, Carrie Wright, Sarah Gorback, Nithiya K. and her composition team at MPS Books, Bruce Emmer, Liz Albritton, and Joanne Farness. My thanks to Zondervan for permission to quote the entire book of Habakkuk in this text. Finally, I am grateful to God for the many blessings I have received while writing this book. I pray that what I have written will be a blessing to others as well.

K.M.K.

ABOUT THE AUTHOR

Kent M. Keith is an author and motivational speaker whose mission is to help people find personal meaning and deep happiness in their lives and work. He has been an attorney, a state government official, a high-tech park developer, a university president, a community organizer, a graduate school lecturer, and a YMCA executive. He is currently the chief executive officer of the Greenleaf Center for Servant Leadership in Indianapolis. He earned a bachelor of arts degree in government from Harvard University, a master of arts in philosophy and politics from Oxford University, a certificate in Japanese from Waseda University, a law degree from the University of Hawaii, and a doctorate in education from the University of Southern California. He is a Rhodes Scholar. Keith and his wife, Elizabeth, have three children. They have lived most of their lives in Honolulu, where he has been a member of Manoa Valley Church for more than thirty years.

For more on *Have Faith Anyway,* visit http://www.paradoxicalchristians.com.